Dov's Mitzvah

by Risa Rotman
illustrated by Ariel Bauer

Dedicated in loving memory of
Chanie Kolodny, a"h,
a young girl whose short life was filled with doing mitzvos, especially for children.

Dov's Mitzvah

Dedicated in memory of our beloved oldest son, Eliyahu Mordechai ben Chaim Yechiel z"l. R.R.

Dedicated l'illuy nishmat Rujama Miriam bat Clara z"l, my beloved mother. A.B.

First Edition - September 2007 / Elul 5767
Copyright © 2007 by HACHAI PUBLISHING
ALL RIGHTS RESERVED

Editor: D.L. Rosenfeld
Managing Editor: Yossi Leverton
Layout: Eli Chaikin

ISBN 13: 978-1-929628-36-0
ISBN 10: 1-929628-36-6
LCCN: 2007930696

HACHAI PUBLISHING
Brooklyn, New York
Tel: 718-633-0100 Fax: 718-633-0103
www.hachai.com info@hachai.com

Printed in China

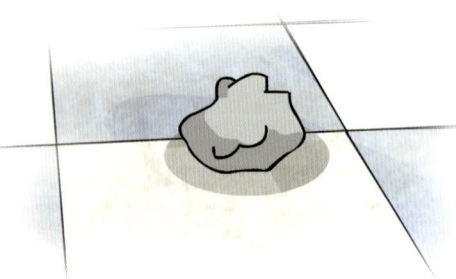

Glossary

Bubby: Grandmother
Mitzvah: One of the 613 commandments; a good deed
Shul: Synagogue
Torah: The law and wisdom contained in the Jewish Scriptures and Oral Tradition; the Five Books of Moses
Yeshiva: School of Torah learning

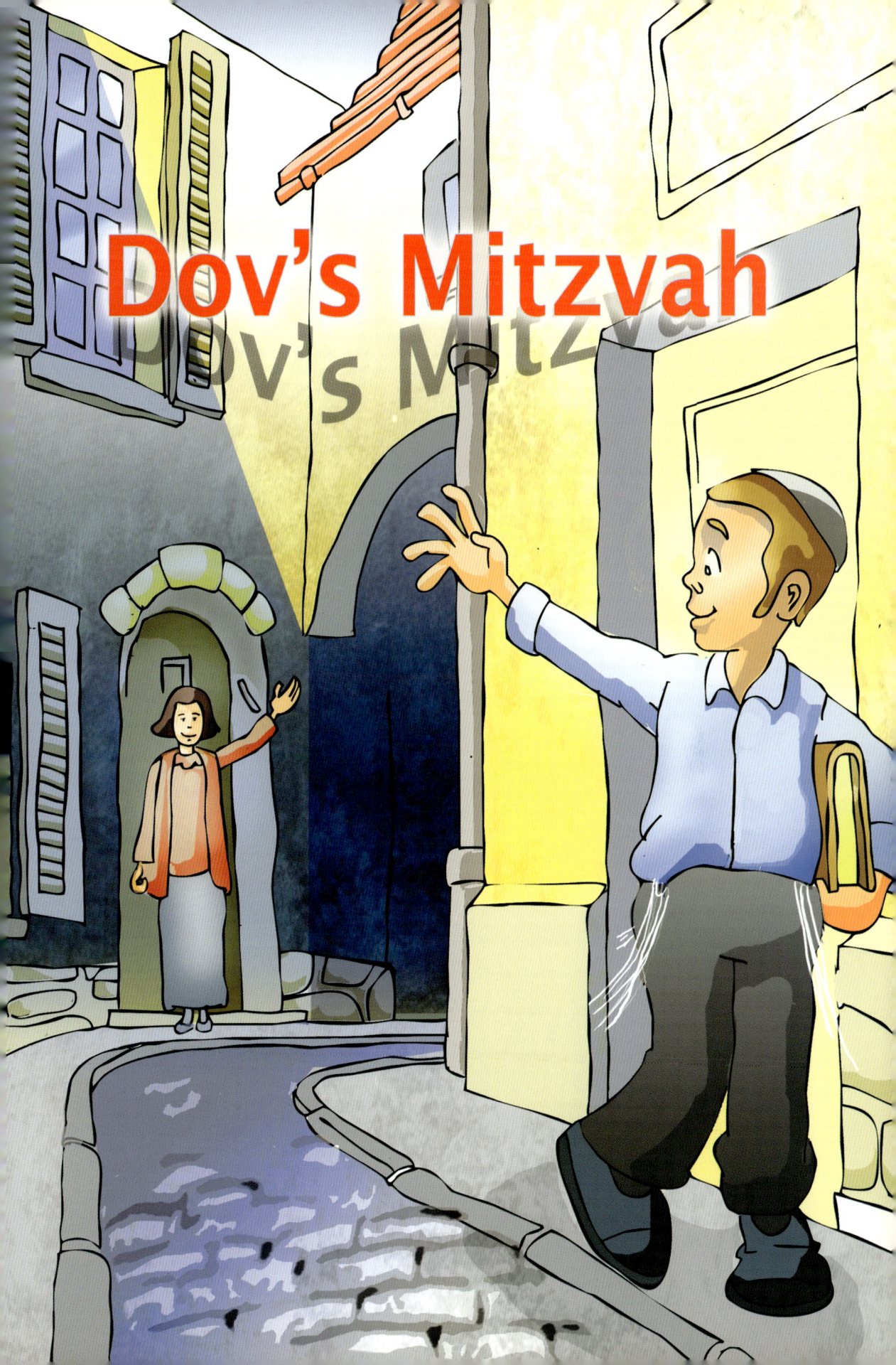

On his way to yeshiva,
Dov saw a big rock,
Right in the path
Where he saw people walk.

"I'm going to move this thing out of the way,
What a nice mitzvah to start off my day!"

Now who should be watching
But Mrs. Steingreen,
Who grew so excited
By what she had seen?

"I won't push it off
'Till I get around to it,
A mitzvah's just waiting
For me to do it!"

"This is my chance to help someone, too,

Now who should be watching
But the bakery man,
On his way down the block
In his bakery van?

"For my special mitzvah, I'm going to bake,

And give a poor couple – a free wedding cake!"

Now who should be watching
But one wedding guest,
Who had an idea
That would not let him rest?

"There's a sad, lonely neighbor that I will invite

For a walk in the park
While it is still light."

Now who should be watching
Right from her classroom,
But a friendly fourth-grader
Named Sarale Bloom?

She looked for a shy girl and asked her to play,

"Will you join me in jump rope at recess today?"

Now who should be watching but Rabbi Gladstone,
Who thought of a mitzvah of his very own?

"I won't push it off 'till I get around to it,
A mitzvah's just waiting for me to do it!"

"I decided to make this last minute call,

To say, 'Let's learn Torah; invite one and all!'"

That evening in shul, a large crowd could be found
So many people had gathered around!

The sound of their learning
Was soothing and sweet.
Dov heard it from his house
That's right down the street!

How surprised he would be to know what you know:
From that mitzvah he did a few hours ago,

Came more and still more... who imagined it would?

Yet one mitzvah can change
The whole world for good.